A BOOK OF
LIBERIAN
PARABLES

A BOOK OF

LIBERIAN PARABLES

WISE SAYINGS AND THEIR SIMPLE INTERPRETATIONS

LULU V. MARSHALL

Archway Publishing books may be ordered through booksellers or by contacting:

Archway Publishing
1663 Liberty Drive
Bloomington, IN 47403
www.archwaypublishing.com
1 (888) 242-5904

Because of the dynamic nature of the Internet, any web addresses or links contained in this book may have changed since publication and may no longer be valid. The views expressed in this work are solely those of the author and do not necessarily reflect the views of the publisher, and the publisher hereby disclaims any responsibility for them.

Any people depicted in stock imagery provided by Thinkstock are models, and such images are being used for illustrative purposes only. Certain stock imagery © Thinkstock.

ISBN: 978-1-4808-2123-1 (sc)
ISBN: 978-1-4808-2124-8 (e)

Library of Congress Control Number: 2015948997

Print information available on the last page.

Archway Publishing rev. date: 09/21/2015

DEDICATION

This book is dedicated to all people of vision (our
parents, grandparents, and great-grandparents)
who put words together that mean even
more today than they did back then.

Freed American slaves founded Liberia in
1847; many of the parables found in this
book emanated from that generation.

To my beloved mother, who during her lifetime gave
unconditional love and care to children and families
in her communities that made a lasting impression
on their lives: for that, I thank you. I extend love and
peace to my precious family for their encouragement
and support in the development of this project to bring
reading enjoyment to people of all walks of life.

Finally, to all who examine this book: may your
knowledge and thinking be enriched as you find
pleasure and understanding from its interpretation.

CONTENTS

CHAPTER 1

———

LIVING

Sedeke (See-dee-key), an architect, was asked to build a house as a thank-you gift for someone who had done a good deed for Gayman, the king.

Sedeke was told to use his free will when determining the cost for the construction. He built the most beautiful house in a few months and turned it over to the king for presentation to his special someone.

Gayman, the king, then called all the people in his kingdom on the day he had set aside for the presentation. I tell you that anybody who was somebody was there that day. At the gathering, Gayman presented the house to Sedeke, the architect, who was very unhappy at receiving it. Everyone wondered why Sedeke was so unhappy at such an important moment in his life.

You see, Sedeke had requested a lot of money for his goods and services, but he had used cheap materials to build the beautiful house.

Moral: Whatever you do in life, good
or bad, you do for yourself.

CHAPTER 2

PARABLES

1. "What man has done, man can still do."
   If it was done before, it can be done again.

2. "You never know the luck of a lousy cat."
   If you don't try, you'll never know.

3. "A dog can measure the throat before swallowing the bone."
   You must know your ability before taking on the task.

4. "Every man knows the pinch of his own shoe."[1]
   Only you can explain how bad your problem is.

5. "Now you know that pepper can burn in a monkey's eye."
   It's nothing when you hurt someone, but when someone hurts you, you think the whole world is coming to an end.

---

[1] Proverbs 14:10.

6. "What can water do to rock?"
   When your spirit is strong, nothing can break it.

7. "Two hills never meet, but people always meet in life."
   Be careful how you treat people, for you may meet them again.

8. "'Come see me' is different from 'come stay with me.'"
   People act differently when they visit than when they live with you.

9. "Open confession is good for the soul."[2]
   You have peace of mind when you admit your faults.

10. "When you point one finger at someone, three fingers point back at you."
    Be careful when you set a trap for someone—you just might fall in.

11. "If sand were sugar, everyone would be drinking tea."
    If all things in life were free, everyone would be rich.

12. "*Korye-Korwolo! (Koo-yee-Koe-wulo)*—You've got eye; you've got heart."[3]
    You see that it's not much, so use your own mind.

13. "Porcupine gut: too bitter to eat, too greasy to throw away."
    He or she is a very likeable person but too much trouble to be around.

---

[2] Psalm 119:26.

14. "Play, play, kill bird."
    After a lot of threats, it will be done.

15. "Put fire on turtle's back."
    Pick up your pace and move fast. [3]

16. "Connie on Connie shoulders."
    You think you're smart, but he's smart too.

17. "Whatever you do in life, you do it for yourself."
    Whatever your deeds are, you will face them in your
    life.

18. "Raccoon knows which stick to rub itself on."
    I may look stupid, but I can fight back.

19. "An eagle can fly high, but it has to come down to
    drink muddy water."
    Be careful who you step on when you're going up;
    you may meet the same person when you're coming
    down.

20. "Every day pitcher go to the well, one day it will
    break."
    You may get away with what you're doing now, but
    one day you will be caught.

21. "If you make your bed hard, you will lie on it hard."
    What you do now will determine your future.

---

[3] Grebo parable (Liberian dialect).

22. "Take time is better than beg pardon."
    Be careful now, and you won't have to apologize later.

23. "A drowning man will hold on to a straw."[4]
    Someone in trouble will take any help he or she can get.

24. "When you enter a village with people beating an old lady, join in, then ask later."
    Don't give opinions without first knowing the facts.

25. "What makes a man shame; makes him mad."
    If you embarrass me, I will fight back.

26. "Good players don't fight for a jersey."
    When you are good, people who know your worth will look for you.

27. "Sarbee (knows his stuff) not got worry."
    If you know your stuff, you don't have to worry; people will find you.

28. "Never burn the bridge that crosses you."
    Never forget where you're coming from; you may need to go back someday.

29. "It's not what you do, but how you do it; it's not what you say, but how you say it."
    Let what you say and what you do be full of grace.

---

[4] Sir Thomas More (1478–1535), "A Dialogue of Comfort against Tribulation" (1534).

30. "You can't hold - sky and shore."
    You may want everything, but you can't have everything.

31. "Free rope who buck it, take it."
    Life is free, so take your chances.

32. "Luck pass fine."
    It's better to be blessed than to be beautiful.

33. "Goat luck is different from sheep luck."
    You may lose at something; another person may win doing the same thing.

34. "Any dirty water can put out fire."
    A hungry man can eat anything.

35. "When two elephants fight, the grass suffers."
    When grown-ups fight, children suffer.

36. "When you pull rope, rope pull bush."
    When you hurt one person, a whole family may be hurt.

37. "Facts come through jokes."
    Jokes tell what people think of you, so listen well.

38. "How you live is how you'll die."
    When you die, people will turn out based on how you lived with them.

39. "If the shoe fits, wear it."[5]
     If you're guilty of what I say, you will react to it.

40. "What will the ox eat while the grass is growing?"
     You cannot wait while I am planning; always have
     an alternative plan.

41. "Life is a stage."[6]
     Do your part with the opportunity you have.

42. "An old broom sweeps clean."
     Stick with what you know; it will serve you better.

43. "Heart ain't got bone."
     People have feelings, so be careful how you treat
     them.

44. "You can't plant okra and reap cassava."
     You reap what you sow.

45. "If you knock nose, eye run water."
     When you hurt one member, the whole family feels it.

46. "Put whip to your horse."
     Move quickly and do what you have to do.

47. "When you're in bat town, you hang like bat."
     When you enter a town, do what the townspeople do.

---

[5] William Shakespeare (1564–1616).
[6] Richard Hooker (1554–1600), *Of the Lawes of Ecclesiasticall Politie* (1593).

48. "Everybody for self, God for all."
     Take care of yourself, and God will take care of the
     rest.

49. "If you listen to the noise of the market, you won't
     buy fish."
     Don't worry about what people think; do the right
     thing.

50. "Steel cut steel."
     You think you are strong, but I am stronger.

51. "*Yarquoi-yarquoi (ya-kwah-ya-kwah)*—Hand go,
     hand come."[7]
     If you take, you must give also.

52. "Poor like a church rat."
     You have nothing like a rat that lives in a church.

53. "One hand can't fill trunk."
     Two people can do a better job than one.

54. "You can't eat crab with shame."
     Tell it like it is.

55. "Don't be like the graveyard."
     Always receiving, never giving.

56. "A leopard can't change its spots."
     You can't change people, so learn to live with them.

---

[7] Grebo (Liberian dialect) parable.

57. "Turtle want fight, but turtle hand short."
    I would like to help, but I'm having trouble myself.

58. "Stop beating around the bush."
    Get straight to the point.

59. "Monkey work, baboon draw."
    You do all the work, and another gets the pay.

60. "I grind arms."
    I agree with you.

61. "Iron self can wear out."
    Don't abuse a person's willingness.

62. "If you play with puppy, it will lick your mouth."
    If you don't respect yourself, no one will respect you.

63. "A shower of rain brings sheep and goats together."
    Problems bring a mix of people together, rich or poor.

64. "Wait, wait kill Roy."
    Don't put off for tomorrow what you can do today.

65. "Black and white can't lie."
    You cannot deny what you've written on paper.

66. "Ninety-nine days for thief but one day for master."
    Whatever is done in secret will one day come to light.

67. "Never let your left hand know what your right hand is doing."[8]
Keep your business to yourself.

68. "Always engage brain before putting mouth in gear."
Think twice before you speak.

69. "Patient dog eats the fattest bone."
Good things come to those who wait.

70. "If house don't sell you, street won't buy you."
If your family members don't talk about you, outsiders won't know.

71. "The just have to suffer with the unjust."
If you hang with troublemakers, you will be punished with troublemakers.

72. "If you don't use your head, your body will suffer."
Think wisely before you act, and you will benefit from your actions.

73. "Don't be led by the nose."
Make your own decisions.

74. "You're too lazy to ache if you had a pain."
You're so lazy that you won't even move a finger to help.

75. "First fool is no fool, but second fool is a big fool."
Don't repeat the same mistake.

---

[8] [8]Matthew 6:3.

76. "Crab with one hole is no crab."
    Always have another plan.

77. "Looking for work and praying not to find it."
    You want work, but you have every excuse not to find it.

78. "Duck or no dinner."
    Either take this or get nothing.

79. "When your hand is in baboon mouth, take time to pull it out."
    When you're in trouble, be careful how you speak to those who want to help.

80. "The half has not been told."[9]
    You haven't heard anything yet.

81. "One hand can't pick lice."
    Two people can do a better job than one.

82. "Kind heart gave nanny-goat short tail."
    You have to do without because you gave away the last you had.

83. "When bad luck calls your name, rotten banana can break your teeth."
    When you're in trouble, those who hate you will add to your problems.

---

[9] The Queen of Sheba, 1 Kings 10:7.

84. "Do what you can and leave the rest to God."
    Do your best, and God will multiply your efforts.

85. "Every day is fishing day, but every day is not catching day."
    If at first you don't succeed, try, try again.

86. "It's better to have something and not need it than to need something and not have it."
    Take care of what you have; you may need it later.

87. "Familiarity breeds contempt and disrespect."[10]
    Being too friendly causes unnecessary talk and bad behavior.

88. "Don't wash your dirty clothes in the front yard."
    Never tell your family secrets to strangers.

89. "A man's best friend is his dollar bill."
    Your money will give you the freedom you need.

90. "You know your friends when you have trouble."
    Real friends stick around when you need them.

91. "When bad luck calls your name, crawfish cut your line."
    When it's not your day, anything can spoil it.

92. "Don't cut your nose to spite your face."
    Don't throw away something you will need later.

---

[10] Aesop (c. 620–564 BC).

93. "Bluff thing ain't got pain."
    A well-dressed person can't feel the pain from his or her shoes.

94. "The water waste but the calabash ain't break."
    You lost what you had, but you can start again.

95. "Hurry, hurry burst trousers."
    Take your time; don't rush.

96. "If you play with fire, it will burn you."
    Stay away from danger; you may get hurt.

97. "Living on a flowery base of ease."[11]
    Do nothing and get everything.

98. "Where you see smoke, fire's there."
    If there's a rumor, there must be a story.

99. "When snake bite you, if you see lizard tail, you will run."
    When you had a bad experience, you'll avoid coming close to it again.

100. "You can't pick up wasted water."
     Cut your losses and move on.

101. "You know where you're born, but you don't know where you'll die."
     Nobody knows the future.

---

[11] Isaac Watts (1674–1748), English hymn writer and theologian.

102. "You say you're pineapple; show your juice."
     Don't boast about your talent; show what you can do.

103. "Car and woman are two things you don't steal in
     life."
     Stealing a car or a woman can bring you trouble.

104. "Misery likes company."[12]
     Miserable people love to see others miserable.

105. "All things are lawful, but all things are not
     expedient."[13]
     Though it may be lawful, it may not be the right
     thing to do.

106. "Sleep has no mercy."
     When you're sleepy, you'll sleep wherever you are.

107. "*Okay* can't spoil business."
     Saying *okay* means nothing unless you do what you
     promise.

108. "I'm the liar; you're the pretty boy."
     I'm telling you the truth, but you don't believe me.

109. "First word go to court; second word go to jail."
     The first thing you say will be held against you.

---

[12] John Ray (1627–1705), English naturalist, philosopher and
theologian
[13] 1 Corinthians 6:12.

110. "Same thing you do to me somebody will do to you."
Be careful when you hurt me; someone will hurt you too.

111. "When my coffee farm gets ripe, I will pay you."
When I can afford it, I will repay your kindness.

112. "You're more a liability than an asset."
I love you, but you cause me too much pain.

113. "Good things not cheap; cheap things not good."
To have something worthwhile, you must pay the price.

114. "Every heart got its own sorrow."
Your problems are different from mine.

115. "What worry you don't worry me."
A big concern of yours may be a small one to me.

116. "He who feels he's too big for the job he has will be too small for the one he wants."[14]
Be satisfied with what you have.

117. "A mind made up is a mind to be feared."
Respect a man's decision, no matter how you feel about it.

118. "Play fool to gain wisdom."[15]
Keep quiet and listen if you want to learn.

---

[14] Sister Edna, St. Teresa's Convent, Monrovia, Liberia.
[15] Proverbs 8:5.

119. "My poor day is buried."
Now I have something I can count on.

120. "Any cry good for burial."
Something, no matter how small, is better than nothing.

121. "You've got the neck, but you don't have the beads."
You have the means, but you don't have the opportunity.

122. "Rat trap not for rat alone."
When you set a trap for someone, remember, it could catch you.

123. "You can't catch black deer in the night."
You must work when it is day, because you cannot see in the night.

124. "The shoe is on the other foot."
Now you understand, because you have the same problem I had.

125. "Birds don't pray for feathers; they pray for long life."
As long as you are alive, you can work to get what you want.

126. "If the green tree is burning, what will the dry one do?"[16]
If you treat your own this way, what will you do to me?

---

[16] Luke 23:31.

127. "It's a broken record."[17]
     I'm tired of hearing the same old story.

128. "If you can't help, don't hurt."[18]
     Keep quiet if you have nothing good to say about
     someone.

---

[17] The Free Dictionary.
[18] Dalai Lama.

CHAPTER 3

LOVING

Unconditional Love

Sando and Kardee were the proud parents of three sons: twins Molly and Amadu, seventeen; and Sardee, sixteen.

Kardee was a very dependable wife and mother. She made sure each day that she did the cooking, washing, cleaning, patching, stacking—you name it, she did it—by the time her family got home.

Sando, a construction worker, dreamed of the day when his three sons would get out of college, marry, have families of their own, and become productive citizens.

Upon graduation from college, Molly decided to travel the world, seeing places and people, never leaving an address for her mother, and sometimes being gone for years at a time. Amadu dropped out of college and got a job selling produce. Sardee decided against going to college, refused to work, and continued to live off his parents.

Through it all, Sando and Kardee prayed for their sons and were always happy and eager when they saw or heard from one of their children. Always wanting to know how they were doing, Sando and Kardee were ready to help when asked and gave advice when needed. They took the time to say the hardest three words—I love you!—which went a far, far way.

Moral: A parent's love can never cease toward a child.

PARABLES

---

1. "Money talks."
   If you have money, you can get whatever you want.

2. "Woman 'kinja' never leave in the street."
   People always have sympathy for a woman in need.

3. "Tongue and teeth can fall out too."
   The best of friends have arguments.

4. "A mother's love can never cease toward her child."[19]
   A mother will always love a child, no matter how bad.

5. "There's no bad bush to throw your child."
   A mother cannot give her bad child to another.

6. "If you can't go through the door, you go through the window."[20]
   If you can't directly get back at the one who hurt you, get back at someone close to him or her.

---

[19] Isaiah 49:15.
[20] Matthew 6:6.

7.   "If it's good for Peter, it's good for Paul."[21]
     If you can have it, I can have it too.

8.   "A parent is never too ugly for his or her child."
     No matter what, a child will always stand up for
     the parent.

9.   "Through crab, crawfish drink water."
     When you have something, share it with someone.

10. "When long teeth man dying, you say he's laughing."
     Someone may tell you about a serious problem, and
     you may think it's a joke.

11. "Before dog ear had sore, fly was eating."
     I was living before you came along.

12. "No tartar baby business here."
     My livelihood doesn't depend only on love.

13. "Birds of the same feather flock together."[22]
     People with the same interests stick together.

14. "No money, no love."
     When the money is finished, love leaves with it.

15. "Cassava leaf not for goat alone."
     Love is free for anyone who can get it.

---

[21] Mark 9:5.
[22] William Turner (1775–1851), *The Rescuing of Romish Fox* (1545).

16. "His eyes are like cassava stick"
    A man is never satisfied—he's always looking here, there, and yonder.

17. "Man was made to ask and woman to accept or reject."
    A man may ask, but a woman has the right to choose.

18. "Baby ain't born yet; the eye crossed."
    I haven't yet agreed to your terms, and you are already trying to own me.

19. "I can't buy pig-in-the-bag."
    You must see and know what you're getting into.

20. "Don't wash your dirty clothes in the street."
    Keep your private life private.

21. "Baby ain't born yet; the eye big so."
    I haven't agreed to your terms, and already you're making big plans.

22. "Water will seek its level."
    A wise man will always find the right group to fit in.

23. "Family stick can bend, but it can't break."
    Family members may disagree, but the ties can never break.

24. "Not because I do you good, you have to do me good."

You don't have to pay me for what I do for you; do good for someone else.

25. "God ain't like ugly, but he made it."
    You do me bad, but someone else will pay you back.

26. "Use your head and not your heart."
    You can't be everything to everyone.

27. "My hand ain't there."
    Don't blame me when it backfires.

28. "Once in Christ never out."
    My old friend will still be my friend down the line.

29. "Old chunk ain't hard to catch."
    Old relationships are easy to start up again.

30. "You're fine, but eh."
    You look good but don't let it go to your head.

31. "That's what friends are for—to inconvenience and embarrass you."
    Your friends will make you go out of your way to help them.

32. "The cows will come home, but when?"
    We know something will happen but not when.

33. "The elephants are crossing the road, and all traffic is stopped,"

When the elders speak, everyone must listen.

34. "Give it a lick and a blow."
I'm doing someone's chores halfway.

CHAPTER 4

CHILD REARING

The Indulgent Mother

The story is told of a single mother who raised her son, Gbachew, who also became the campus bully at school. He brought home expensive clothes and lots of money when he didn't have a job, but his mother never asked where those things had come from or had him return them.

Gbachew dropped out of school, complaining to his mother that nobody liked him, and she didn't try to find out what the problem was. She agreed that it was all right to leave school since no one cared about him anyway. He soon began a life of crime.

At the age of thirty, Gbachew was arrested, tried, convicted, and sentenced to death by hanging for robbing and killing a man. Yeda, his mother, was grief stricken; she began to lose weight and her appetite for living because of the situation with her only child.

When Gbachew was on his way to the gallows, someone asked him whether he wanted anything. His only wish was to speak to his mother, who was in the back of the crowd. As she made her way to the front, Gbachew also drew closer to her. Upon reaching his mother, Gbachew embraced Yeda and whispered in her ear, "If you had only told me when I was wrong, this would not be happening; however, whenever you see your ear, you will always remember me." He then let go of her and said he was ready to be hanged.

Yeda bled from the right ear, which her son had bitten off. She lost her son that day and was forced to live the rest of her life with one ear.

Moral: Spare the rod and spoil the child.[23]

---

[23] Proverbs 13:24.

The Facts of Life[24]

Years ago, a six-year-old was late for dinner. After frantically calling the neighbors in the building with kids his age, his father finally located him and got him on the phone.

Frustrated with anxiety and concern, and upset with his lateness, his father angrily asked, "Do you know what time it is?"

After a moment of silence, he heard the small voice asking the parents of his friend, "Excuse me, my father wants to know the time."

The father immediately realized his anger hadn't communicated and had had no effect. It was the wrong time and the wrong manner to get through to the child.

It is believed that every child gives a parent the opportunity to work on and improve one (or more) of his or her own character traits, such as frustration and anger. Being a parent can be trying, but the rewards are great. There is an old Yiddish saying: "Small children, small problems; big children, big problems; small children, small opportunities; big children, big opportunities." It is the only job you're out of by the time you're trained.

Moral: A parent's job is never done.[24]

---

[24] With permission from Rabbi Kalman Packouz, Shabbat Shalom Weekly, http://www.shabbatshalom.org.

PARABLES

----

1.   "Frisky bird mess in the nest."
   If you show off, you will be embarrassed.

2.   "Praise a white chicken, and it will dirty its feathers."
   Just when you praise me, I spoil everything.

3.   "Fuss don't born good babies"
   When you're mad, you say things you regret later.

4.   "When someone leaves home, the first thing the person packs is his or her ways."
   No matter where a person goes, it's not long before he or she shows his or her real self.

5.   "The child who says his or her mother will not sleep; will not sleep also."
   A stubborn child will be punished.

6.   "Thank God for little favors."
   Be thankful for what you've got.

7. "Thank God for this mouthful; hope the next one will be a meal."
    Eat this small one now, and a full meal will come later.

8. "If you make yourself grass, the cows will eat you."
    If you sell yourself cheap, people will buy you cheap.

9. "The song the children are singing in the court-yard is the topic the grown-ups are discussing in the parlor."
    Be careful when you gossip about others; children are listening.

10. "One cent can't make noise."
    One person cannot have a quarrel.

11. "Because my mama is sick, I don't have to kiss the doctor's toes."
    Although I need your help, I don't have to take your insults.

12. "When little boy says he will chunk you, he's already got his rock."
    When I say I will do something, I've already thought it through.

13. "The child who can't sit down won't see the mother's grave."
    Staying out will cause you to miss out on important things.

14. "Crab that can't stop crawling will soon fall into the pot."
    If you don't sit and be quiet, you'll soon get into trouble.

15. "Moon walk, till day break on it."
    If you continue to do wrong, you'll soon be caught.

16. "Eat breakfast till dinner is ready."
    Be content with what you have until you can do better.

17. "Little boy can run, but he can't hide."
    Whatever you do in the dark, will come to light.

18. "Baby crawls before it walks."
    Take it easy; don't rush in life.

19. "A schoolmaster was once a schoolboy."
    A parent was once a child and knows all the tricks.

20. "If little boy knocks you small, knock him hard."
    Don't allow your child to hit you when he or she is little, or your child will hit you when he or she is grown.

21. "Don't let people eat off your head."
    Stand up for yourself, or people will take advantage of you.

22. "If I plant you, will you grow?"

If I ask you to do something, will you do it?

23. "Pig now grow hog."
    I knew you when you were a baby; now you're all grown up.

24. "Child, don't stay on man hand long time."
    Before you know it, a child grows out of the crib into a man.

25. "Before good food waste, let belly burst."
    You don't need it, but because you see it, you must have it.

26. "Show me your friends, and I'll tell you who you are."[25]
    You are judged by the company you keep.

27. "You na hear doodoo speak meggan."
    Don't believe anything he says.

28. "If you don't work, you don't eat."[26]
    You must work to enjoy the good things of life.

29. "Cut your coat according to your cloth."[27]
    Live within your means.

30. "Never take a man by his looks."

---

[25] Proverbs 13:20.

[26] 2 Thessalonians 3:10.

[27] Irish proverb.

Don't form opinions of others; take time to get to know them.

31. "The age of Methuselah has nothing to do with the wisdom of Solomon."[28]
A youth can give an elder sound advice.

32. "'Never' belongs to God."
Only God can say "never."

33. "Small shame is better than big shame."
The little people know about you is enough.

34. "We can all sing together, but we can't all talk together."
Talk one at a time to understand each other.

35. "Please give me elbow room."
Give me some space and stop looking over my shoulder.

36. "Now you're cooking with gas."
Now that's the right thing to say.

37. "Sell it like I bought it."
Tell it like it is.

38. "Big boy shoe, small boy can't wear."
Small people shouldn't do things big people do.

---

[28] Genesis 5:25.

39. "Crabby like a setting hen"
    You react to everything.

40. "'Please lend me,' looks like 'Please give me.'"
    Borrowing something and keeping it.

41. "Hang your hat where your hand can reach it."
    Don't overextend yourself.

42. "No name, no blame."
    I didn't call your name, so you can't blame me.

43. "Clip your wings."
    Put you in your place.

44. "You hang around until they hang up the last dishcloth."
    When you visit, you don't know when to leave.

45. "Lean where the wind blows."
    Always jumping to the sides where you can benefit.

46. "You smell the rat."
    You've come to your senses.

47. "If ain't there, ain't there."
    If you don't know it, you just don't know it.

48. "The same clock that strikes midnight strikes midday."
    Things may be hard today, but may be better tomorrow.

49. "Going to goat house for wool."
     Asking the wrong person for advice.

50. "John's palm oil waste on John's rice."
     You did it to yourself; I can't put my mouth in it.

51. "Did the cat carry your tongue?"
     Now you are so quiet; can you talk at all?

52. "You have to walk chalk line."
     Be careful with what you say or do.

53. "People don't 'mean' you with news."
     You don't have to ask; people will tell you what they know.

54. "Drop it like hot cake."
     Leave the situation quickly.

55. "Got no one to bury you and forcing yourself to die."
     Bringing more problems on yourself than you can solve.

56. "When you have teeth, you must chew bones; and when you have money, you must use it."
     Take advantage of every opportunity you get.

57. "Sucking air."
     Catching a hard time.

58. Burn your wire."
     I will make the connection for you.

CHAPTER 5

SHORT STORIES AND WISE SAYINGS

Street Car Washer

There once lived a man named Tyler, who could be seen in Monrovia on Benson Street, Broad Street, Center Street, or even on Lynch Street at any given hour of the day.

Tyler was a tall man, standing about five feet eleven inches, who had a reputation for "washing" people's cars voluntarily. He targeted motorists who stopped for the red light. Tyler appeared with a cloth and began to clean the windshield on the driver's side of the car.

To quickly get rid of him, drivers shelled out a few dollars or cents to compensate for his unwanted service.

Because of Tyler's shabby appearance—dirty clothes and sometimes no shoes or a worn-out pair of "pop-pop" slippers—no one took him seriously.

But when he died and a friend placed an obituary in the local newspaper, he revealed that Tyler had been a married man and the father of several children who had done well for themselves by going to school and becoming purposeful members of society; and that Tyler was the owner of five houses, four of which had been rented out to tenants.

Moral: Never take a man by his looks.

Son, Read Your Bible

When Dada left home for college, his father gave him a Bible and told him to always read it for God's protection and provision of anything he would ever need. Each time Dada called home, he told his parents how much he enjoyed his Bible reading.

At the end of his second week at school, Dada called his father and asked for fifty dollars to buy some school supplies. The father asked, "Are you reading your Bible, Son?"

He was quick to answer, "Oh yes, Dad, and I'm enjoying every minute of it."

The father said, "Son, read your Bible."

The son continued to call and complain month after month about what he didn't have, and each time his father's response was the same: "Son, read your Bible."

Frustrated and at his wit's end, the son returned home to his parents and announced he had decided to quit school because he couldn't cope with not having a lot of what he needed to function as a student. At this point the father asked to see his Bible. The frustrated son pulled out the dust-covered Bible from among his belongings. The father proceeded to open the Bible. Behind the first page was a hundred-dollar bill, followed by another hundred at the end of each chapter. The son was most embarrassed to find that all the time he'd been complaining, he'd had everything he ever really needed.

Moral: You do good, you do it for yourself.

False Teeth: Why They Fall Out

Spider was a close neighbor of Ma Joe. One day Spider was invited to a party in the city, but he didn't have any teeth and suspected that a lot of people would be around to see him. So he decided to borrow Ma Joe's false teeth. Ma Joe agreed to let Spider use the teeth, but he had to return them early the next morning.

The next morning Ma Joe had to attend a PTA meeting at the children's school, but Spider had not returned her false teeth. She sent for the teeth, but Spider wasn't home and left a note promising that he would deliver them as soon as possible.

Ma Joe waited for one hour, then two hours, but Spider was not in sight. As a result Ma Joe decided to go get the false teeth herself. On the way Spider met her, and in her haste to put the false teeth on, they wouldn't stay and kept falling out. The problem was that Spider had resized the false teeth to fit his own mouth.

Moral: Don't cut your nose and spoil your face.

Waiting for Jesus

Mr. Josiah was a very devout Christian who believed Jesus would surprisingly come back again. So Mr. Josiah began to prepare himself each day to welcome Jesus.

On the day rumors said Jesus was expected in town, Mr. Josiah realized he didn't have any milk for coffee in case Jesus stopped by and needed to drink a cup. So he went out to buy some milk.

On his way to the grocery store, just as he stepped outside his door, he met a shabbily dressed man asking for money to buy something to eat. Mr. Josiah quickly brushed by him and continued his walk to the store. As he reached the front of the grocery store, an old lady confronted him, asking for a quarter. Again he said he was in a hurry and had no money.

Mr. Josiah bought the milk and ran back home. Upon entering the house, he rushed to answer a ringing phone, and the voice on the other end asked, "What did Jesus say when you met him?" Mr. Josiah said he hadn't met Jesus. The voice said to him, "You talked to him twice on your way out." Mr. Josiah asked, "How can that be when Jesus hasn't yet come?" Mr. Josiah then remembered meeting the shabby old man and the old lady begging alms.

Moral: Be kind to whomever you meet, for
"some have entertained angels unaware."[29]

---

[29] Hebrews 13:2 (KJV).

The Black Rose

There was a very nice man who was a king, and he became ill. The kingdom was in an uproar, and the best doctors in the world were sent for to diagnose and treat the king's case. They found out that the only thing that could save the king's life was a black rose. The only place such a rose could be found was in the valley below a mountain where giants lived, and these giants killed anyone who dared to go there.

The king's men were told, and they decided that no matter what, they would go and pick the needed rose to save their king. Upon reaching the top of the mountain, they looked down and saw the beautiful black roses growing everywhere in the valley. The only problem was getting to them without the giants seeing them.

In that instance, a little boy appeared and asked what they were doing there. When they told him their story, he said he always picked the roses. They asked him to go down and pick one for them. He agreed but said they would have to hold the rope that would take him down; then, when the giants were coming toward him, they would need to pull him back up. The townspeople agreed, but the little boy didn't trust his life to them and said he would run home and get his father to hold the rope. He said, "When things get rough and the giants are coming, you will let go of the rope, but I know that no matter how rough it may get, my father will not leave me there."

Moral: Can a parent's love ever cease
toward his or her child?

Sweet Mother Heels

The fashion in town was platform shoes, and they were called "sweet mother heels." To be in things, John bought himself a pair of sweet mother heels that were five inches high. What he didn't know was that one should practice walking in these shoes before trying to wear them outside the home.

One Sunday John dressed like a drunk to go out on the town. Unfortunately, he had difficulty walking in his shoes. It was fun to watch him hold onto the wall or anyone, even a child, who was nearby. When he entered the yard, there was no wall or person to hold on to, so he had to take one step at a time, when he could normally take three. John finally decided to go back into the house, kick off his sweet mother heels, and put on his regular shoes, with which he needed no help walking.

Moral: Old broom sweeps clean.

The Traveler and the Drum

Gussie was traveling back to Liberia from a trip to Nairobi, Kenya, where she had bought a few gift items, including a large African drum. Upon her arrival at the Jomo Kenyatta International Airport, she was shocked to find three check-in counters open with winding lines, each two to three miles long. She stood with her hands folded. The bad part about this was that her flight was only thirty minutes away from being called, and standing in line would take a much longer time.

Upon getting out of the taxi, she stood in awe and was deciding whether to join a line or return to the hotel and try for the next flight, when someone approached her—maybe the airport cleaner, someone who hung around the airport, an undercover agent, or a robber. I guess, but who knows? So she held on tightly to her pocketbook.

The man asked, "Are you going?"

Gussie answered, "I want to, but look at those lines."

He said to her, "Wait here. I'll be right back." In less than two minutes, he was back with a trolley. He began loading her luggage and the drum, and he told her to follow him. They went up to a station that read CLOSED, and he told her to wait there. In another few minutes he was back with a female attendant, who took her passport and ticket, processed them, returned them to her, and said, "Have a nice flight."

After that, the attendant closed the station and returned to the area from which the man had brought her. The man then took Gussie to the VIP lounge and gave her a seat. Still awe stricken, Gussie couldn't believe this was all happening to her. She opened her pocketbook (the same one she had tightly held earlier) and gave him all the remaining French francs she had—maybe ten dollars or less—and said, "Thank you."

The man asked her, "Did I pay my dues?" She couldn't even answer the question. Because of what he had done for her, she felt she could never come close to paying her dues. He left, and a few minutes later, Gussie boarded the plane, never to see the man again in her lifetime.

Moral: Never take a man by his looks.

Dog's Nose

Mr. Dog was dating to marry Cattie, the sister of Dr. Cat. One day Dr. Cat, a plastic surgeon, told his sister that Mr. Dog's nose was too big and needed some work done before the wedding.

The next day, when Mr. Dog was visiting, Cattie told him she didn't like the size of his nose and said it would be a good idea to have it made smaller before the wedding. Because of his love for Cattie, Mr. Dog agreed to have Dr. Cat, his future brother-in-law, do the work as soon as possible.

Dr. Cat, so anxious to make his sister's future husband look his very best, cut too much off the nose and made it short. Upon seeing the short nose, Cattie refused to marry Mr. Dog and despises him to this day. This is why a dog cannot stand to see a cat.

Moral: Never change for anyone; it pays to be yourself.

The Man and the Barrel

One day as Mr. Johnson was taking his afternoon siesta, a lot of noise in his front yard rudely awoke him. Upon investigating the noise, he found out that his house was on fire.

Mr. Johnson jumped out of bed and rushed to the back of his house, where he kept a fifty-two-gallon water barrel. He picked up the barrel, ran with it to the front of the house, put the fire out, and then put the barrel down.

When Mr. Johnson needed to take the empty barrel to the other side of the house, where he'd taken it from in the first place, he asked for help because he said the barrel was too heavy to carry alone.

Moral: You never know what you can do until you do it.

The Visitor

One afternoon Sister went home early from work to spend time with Grand, who was ill.

When Sister entered the room, Grand introduced her to a man who had come to visit her. The man told Sister he was a medical doctor working with the Firestone Medical Center in Harbel, Liberia, and was being transferred to the John F. Kennedy Hospital in Monrovia. He said he had rented a home in Grand's neighborhood on Duport Road and was moving in with his family, who would soon come to town. After a brief conversation, the doctor quickly left.

Grand told Sister that the doctor had promised to bring his family, when they came to town from Harbel, so they could pray together. But Grand wanted to pray with him first. So she asked Sister to call him back. Sister and a neighbor went looking for where the stranger said he had moved, but there was no new building in the area; no neighbors seemed to know him. This, of course, was a mystery to everyone, especially when the stranger never returned as promised.

Moral: Be nice to people; you never know
whom you may be entertaining.

The Driver and the Turn

Zoe had recently graduated from the local driving school and was carefully practicing her driving skills when late one evening, in an emergency, she was called upon to drive her mother and two sisters to a relative's home.

She had driven about ten minutes when Zoe met her family walking toward her. Her mother asked her to turn the car around so they could get in and continue the ride. The situation was funny when Zoe, overcome with emotion, announced that she couldn't turn the car around and didn't know how to drive.

Although her family coaxed and encouraged her, no amount of teaching or coaching could help rebuild Zoe's confidence. Her older sister had to take over and drive. Everyone was happy, and the trip was completed.

Moral: Always have another plan, such
as a second driver. It helps.

Two Old Men on a Cold Night

Being in the tropics, Liberians enjoy warm weather year-round. However, during the months between November and February in Yekepa, a city in the northern part of Nimba County, the temperature is unusually cold. This kind of weather is also experienced in the capital city, Monrovia, during the Christmas and New Year season. Then a sweater or some other type of heavy clothing is required at night or in the early morning hours. In some cases, however, it isn't enough, no matter how warm your clothing may be.

On one of these cold nights in Yekepa, two old men lay sleeping in a corner on the sidewalk—they were homeless. Suddenly, in the middle of the night, one man could hardly move because of poor blood circulation. The other man rubbed his friend's limbs to keep him alive, and in so doing, he kept his own blood in circulation and saved his life.

Moral: To get you must give.

The Milk Bottle

John had to attend a very important gathering on Friday, where he was supposed to meet with some investors. A strange feeling overpowered him when he couldn't find the iron, since he had used it with the ironing board only a few moments before.

He retraced his steps to find where he had put the iron. He looked in the closet where the ironing board stays, and guess what he found? A bottle of milk.

John laughed at himself and went straight to the refrigerator. Upon opening the door, he found the iron in a neat sitting position, smiling at him. Okay, now he had found the iron, but where was the ironing board?

Moral: Don't laugh—anyone can make a mistake.

Best Friends

In the afternoon heat, Joe Momo brought home a stolen cow. You see, he thought he had committed the "perfect" crime and that no one knew about his theft.

However, Joe thought his best friend, Peter, could keep his secret and decided to tell him. Joe told Peter that he had something to tell him, but Peter had to promise not to tell anyone. Peter promised that he would keep the secret. Joe then told Peter and asked him whether he had a best friend other than him. Peter said yes; John was his other best friend.

So Joe visited John and invited him to the party he was planning. Again, Joe asked John whether he had another best friend, and he said Martie. Joe visited Martie, told her the same thing, and asked whether she had a best friend. Martie said her best friend was Sam. Joe then visited Sam, told him he was planning a party, and extended an invitation for him to attend. Joe asked Sam whether he had a best friend, and Sam said yes; his best friend was Sackie. Joe visited Sackie and invited him to the party.

On the day of the party, they all sat around the table, where a large covered platter of "something" sat. Joe introduced the occasion and wondered aloud whether anyone could tell him what was under the cover. All hands went up, and together they said, "Cow meat."

Moral: Don't tell anyone what you don't
want other people to know.

Going Crazy

Two ladies visited a doctor's office, hoping to have children of their own. The doctor informed them that to have children, they would have to give up something. He asked them whether they were prepared "to go crazy."

One lady returned home sad because she wasn't prepared to give up her sanity. The other lady went on to have two children, one right after the other, but she didn't go crazy. She, however, seemed to lose something. When her children were at age one, she was coaxing and begging. When they were five and eight, she was yelling, "Put it down and move away from there." By their teenage years, the mother was like, "Clean up your room. Wash the dishes. Move that. I told you to be back by ten p.m. I can't take this."

Seeing that her friend hadn't gone crazy, the second woman revisited the doctor to find out why he had said they would go crazy. The doctor told her that going crazy didn't literally mean going crazy but that she had to be ready to act as if she was going crazy.

Moral: Don't believe everything you hear.[30]

---

[30] 1 John 4:1.

The Man and the Teller

One morning a man wearing a pair of farmers' overalls walked into the bank and stood in line for service. When it was his turn, he asked the teller for a manager's check in the amount of $1 million to be made in his favor. The disgusted teller asked him to stand aside for the next customer to be served.

After waiting an hour without being served, the man told the teller to forget about his request and asked to see the president of the bank. The man was then informed that the president was very busy and couldn't see him. The man in the farmers' overalls left the bank without being served.

Upon returning home, he called the bank president and told him he was closing all his accounts. When asked why, he told the president he'd visited the bank that morning only to test the system and see how an ordinary person was being treated. He said he was surprised to find there was no respect for the ordinary person at a bank where he had invested so much. He didn't want to continue his association with them.

You see, the man in the overalls was a humanitarian and the billionaire who'd kept this particular bank running.

Moral: Be careful who you step on during your way up; you may have to meet him or her on your way down.[31]

---

[31] Wilson Mizner (1876–1933).

The Man in the Tree

A man thought he was the least in the world because he had no food to eat, no clothes to wear, no friends to talk to, and no place to sleep. He just felt down each day of his life.

One day he decided to end his suffering by committing suicide. After thinking the matter through, he went into the woods and climbed a palm tree. He had a banana someone had given him along the way. When he dropped the banana peel, someone picked it up and began eating the peel.

Next, he took off his clothes and threw them down before jumping from the tree. A naked man, who had been hiding himself behind the tree, grabbed the clothes and put them on.

Finally, the man thought, *Huh ... If someone can eat the peel I dropped and another doesn't even have clothes to wear and would be happy to take the rags I don't want, I may not be the least in the world after all.*

After this, his thinking became, *If I live, my condition could change for the better, but if I kill myself, I will never know what might have been.* Immediately the man got down from the tree and went home with the renewed hope of starting over again.

Moral: No condition is permanent.

Why Didn't the Man Get the Job?

Suma, a young professional, met Mr. Venet, a large corporation owner, through the introduction of his classmate and friend, the owner's son. Immediately, the older man became interested in talking to the energetic young man and invited him to lunch.

The next day at the set time and place, Suma met Mr. Venet, who entertained him with a sumptuous lunch. Mr. Venet used this time to find out a little more about Suma, since he felt there was the possibility of offering this promising young man a job in his company.

The working lunch was successful, and Mr. Venet shook hands with Suma and told him it was nice meeting and talking with him. The older man pushed in his chair and departed.

Later that day, when Mr. Venet got home, he had a conversation with his son and told him he thought he could use Suma as his personal assistant at the office. However, he was disappointed that Suma had shown poor manners during their meeting. Mr. Venet said that Suma had reached across the table several times during their lunch and had left his chair away from the table at the end of the meal. For these reasons, he thought employing him would be a bad idea.

Moral: Watch your manners; others are watching you.

The Dog and the Car Tire

Long ago, when a dog was a general mechanic, he was contracted to repair a car tire. Mr. Dog worked hard to repair the car and put it back on the road.

When he was certain the car was again in good running condition, Mr. Dog requested payment for his services. But the car owner refused to pay him and made excuses to Mr. Dog each time he saw him.

Mr. Dog became very hurt and decided to dislike all car tires. To this day, each time a dog sees a running car, he or she runs and barks after it. If the car is parked, he or she pees on the tire.

Moral: A man must be paid for the work he does.

The Princess and The Prince

There once lived a princess who wanted to get married but only if she could find a handsome prince. Her father, who was king, sent out a team to search for a man worthy to be his son-in-law.

The princess rejected everyone the team found, because she found some fault with his looks. One day as the princess was walking in the woods, she met the man of her dreams—a handsome and flawless man. She took him home to her father and told the king this was the man she wanted to marry.

The wedding plans were made, and they married in the palace. During the ceremony, the prince told the gathering he had a secret and would now like to reveal it since he was marrying his princess. Everyone was at attention when he said he was really a frog who had changed into whatever he wished based on the particular situation in which he found himself.

He then changed to a frog and hopped up to kiss his bride, who by now had fainted and had to be carried out of the hall.

Moral: It is never good to pick and choose.

The Kind Fisherman

There once lived a man in Sowah Town, Marshall County, whose name was Fisherman Al. He loved fishing and cared so much for his townspeople that he made it a custom to go fishing every day to help feed the town.

Fisherman Al, as he was affectionately called, came home late each night with a large quantity of fish, but he always took the time to divide it into packages for every home before taking his rest. Each evening the wives all waited anxiously for his return to cook the family dinner.

Several times Fisherman Al invited the men of the town to come along with him so he could teach them how to fish. They were all reluctant and didn't feel it was a good idea, since they could remain at home, and whatever he caught and brought back would feed them.

One Friday Fisherman Al became ill and couldn't work for a whole month. The townsmen were unable to provide meat for their families, and this lack soon became a big problem. They couldn't afford to buy meat for their families, and some began losing weight.

Fisherman Al died. The town was without a provider of meat, because everyone who could have learned to fish had refused to learn.

Moral: Give them fish, and they'll eat sometimes; teach them to fish, and they'll eat all the time.

The Frozen Snake

One day after a brief and heavy snowstorm, Helen traveled home. She saw a belt—or something that looked like one—lying in the ice. She decided to stop and pick it up. After careful examination, she discovered it was a snake that had become frozen from the cold. Upon reaching home, she decided to nurse the snake back to health and keep it as her pet.

When the snake was well and itself again, the lady decided to play with her pet. Guess what? It bit her.

Surprised, she asked the snake, "Why did you do that after all I have done for you?"

The snake replied, "Didn't you know I am a snake and that I bite?"

Moral: A snake is a snake, frozen or unfrozen.

The Proud Frog

Mr. Frog became sick with boils all over his body. The local doctors did all they could, but Mr. Frog didn't get well.

One day a faraway friend came to visit and told him about a doctor in a city, the distance of two days' walk. This was trouble! As you know, Mr. Frog hopped, and his condition would slow him down, more so the trip of two days would take over a week.

After "hanging head" with all his concerned friends, he decided that his best bet was to fly. But he didn't have wings, and an airplane wouldn't take him. Then a clever thought came to his mind. If two of his friends from the bird family held either end of a stick, he could hold onto the middle with his mouth and reach the doctor.

His bird friends agreed to take him. The trip was planned, and their journey started early the next morning.

However, halfway through the trip, people looking up from the ground and seeing them wondered who had come up with such a brilliant idea. Mr. Frog, puffed up with pride, opened his mouth and shouted back, "I did!" And he fell to his death.

Moral: Pride goes before the fall.[32]

---

[32] Proverbs 16:18.

Mr. Spider's Waist

Have you ever wondered why Mr. Spider's waist is so small?

Well, Mr. Spider and his family lived in Toad Town, next to Farm Town in Grand Gbessie County. He had many friends in both towns and was a man given to a large appetite.

Once, a wedding in Toad Town and a country cook in Farm Town were planned on the same day, and Mr. Spider, being their good friend, was invited to both events. However, not knowing the time of the events, he decided to attend both and tied a rope around his waist, giving an end to each town. When the party was ready, his friends would pull on their end, and he would know which direction to go.

Unfortunately, the parties began at the same time, and the rope pulled in both directions. Toad Town continued pulling hard because Mr. Spider didn't respond. Farm Town did the same. Mr. Spider's waist became smaller and smaller as the townspeople pulled on the rope from both sides.

Finally, Mr. Spider's waist was so small and his energy so spent that he fainted. The towns were called to loosen their hold on the rope. The damage had already been done, and Mr. Spider's waist couldn't be repaired.

Moral: Don't wish for everything your eyes see.

The Boy and the Old Man

A little boy went out to play in the woods on a sunny day and caught a bird. While returning home, he met an old man.

After starting a conversation, the little boy asked the old man whether he could tell him what he had in his hand.

The old man replied, "I don't know. You have it in your hand."

"Yes, but what is it?" the boy asked.

The old man said again, "I don't know. You have it in your hand, and you can do whatever you wish with it."

Then the little boy said, "It is a bird, but can you tell me if it is dead or alive?"

The old man said, "No, I can't tell you because you have it in your hand. If I say it is dead, you will open your hand, and it will fly away. If I say it is alive, you will squeeze it, and it will die. The life is in your hand. Do as you see fit."

Moral: You have the power to do anything
you want to do—good or evil.

The Auction

A rich man, whose wife had died a few years before he did, had one son. The son became physically handicapped and needed help in moving about. However, he enjoyed painting. The man loved his son very much and saw him as the most beautiful child in the world.

One day the son died and left his grieving father with only one painting. Each morning the father viewed the painting on the wall. The father died and left instructions that everything he owned should be auctioned off.

The day of the auction came, and the auctioneer first put up the son's painting. He asked whether anyone would pay one hundred dollars for the painting—"Going once, going twice!—and no one took it. He tried again. An old man, the former gardener of the rich man, stood up and offered twenty dollars. The auctioneer again asked for a higher price. When the audience gave no response, he packed up his wares.

At this juncture, someone from the audience yelled out in protest, "We are still waiting to bid on the other items."

The auctioneer told them, "You just don't understand. The auction is over. The father left strict instructions that whoever bought his son's painting took everything else he had left."

Moral: Good things come in small packages.

Why Did the Boy Kick the Dog?

It was the dry season, and the beautiful leaves were yellow. The leaves fell off the trees and covered the ground all around the yard.

When John's father came out of the house and prepared to go for a morning walk, he was surprised to see so many leaves lying around. He decided to give John the chore of raking up the leaves when he returned home from school on Tuesday afternoon.

After accepting the duty, John came home, did his homework, and decided to go out and play with his friends for a little while. However, this turned out to be a long while.

When John's father returned home from work on Tuesday afternoon and found the chores not done, he was very upset and gave John a good talking to.

Unhappy with his father's scolding, John went out and kicked the dog.

Moral: Follow the rule and avoid the conflict.

Third Street Rivals

Across from each other, on Third Street in Middletown, lived two friends, Johnny and Nathan. These two 'friends' were blessed with wealth and all life could give them, but they were never satisfied because of their jealousy of each other.

If Johnny bought a new car, Nathan went out, bought five new cars, and parked them all in his front yard. When Nathan painted his house, Johnny painted his house and even the pavement.

After observing the situation with concern for a while, the Good Lord sent an angel to find out why the two friends couldn't see eye to eye and were so jealous of each other after all the blessings they had received. The angel also said, "Johnny, the Lord would like to know what you would like if you could have one wish granted. But remember that whatever you wish for, your friend Nathan will have twice as much."

Johnny thought for a long while and then replied, "I wish he would strike me blind in one eye!"

Moral: Be thankful for what you have.

ABOUT THE AUTHOR

Lulu V. Marshall, a Liberian-American and resident of the United States for more than twenty-five years, studied in Liberia and the United States, has enjoyed a lengthy career both as a secretary and as part of the insurance industry, and encourages people to read and to embrace positive motivation.